CW00373177

MOTOR DO'S AND DON'TS

MOTOR
DO'S AND DON'TS

BY
HAROLD PEMBERTON
"DAILY MAIL" MOTORING CORRESPONDENT

EBURY
PRESS

TO
ALL TRUE LOVERS OF
THIS HAPPY AND HEALTHY PASTIME
BOTH PRESENT AND
TO BE

First Published in 1923
This edition published in 2008

MOTOR DO'S AND DON'TS

MOTORING

FOR motoring purposes the inhabitants of Great Britain can be divided into two classes— the people who own motor-cars and the people who envy those who own motor-cars. To the latter my wish is that they may speedily obtain the wherewithal to become the former.

At the time of writing this book British manufacturers are turning out new cars at the rate of about one every quarter of an hour, while in the United States the birthrate of motor-cars is about one a minute.

The popularity of motoring grows as quickly as the prosperity of a country allows.

Now that the lean years of the war are passing, the motor industry is rapidly reviving in this country. The real motoring age is only just beginning. Every day there is an increasing number of recruits to the merry brotherhood which throngs the gay " open road."

For this reason also motoring is becoming more dangerous. In capable hands a motor-car is safe enough, but unfortunately the hands are not always capable. If the part of this book which deals with driving, and road chivalry, savours of preaching, this is my excuse.

Some err through ignorance. Good driving, road sense, a subtle term which covers the almost psychic sense of risks you can or can not take, can only be learned through experience—though this little book of mine is intended to assist the beginner in these matters.

As for the confirmed " Road Hog," he is past conversion. He may read the " DON'TS " which I have set out, but for him they will be " DO's." I have not dealt with the highly technical side of the motor-car. This book is not intended to be a Motoring Manual. There are plenty of such works available.

But an effort has been made to lay bare in the simplest of language that side of a motor-car's life which should not remain a secret to the owner-driver, while omitting that which calls for the attention of the skilled mechanic.

We will now buy our car.

CHOOSING A MOTOR-CAR

When the news has got abroad that you are going to buy a motor-car—you may yourself in a moment of pride have dropped the hint—your motoring friends will crowd to your assistance.

You will probably find that they will heartily recommend the particular car which they drive themselves.

If you are going to rely upon the advice of a friend, listen to the one who has owned one make of car for a number of years. Do not rush to buy a similar car to the one which Mr. Smith bought last week, and which he declares is the finest thing in motor-cars that ever took the road. Any motor-car owner with any sense of pride will tell you that his is the *Best Car in the world*. Unless you are an expert it is unadvisable to speculate with an entirely new model ; it may be good, but, on the other hand, after a year on the road faults in design may develop. If you are not an expert and cannot judge an engine and a good chassis when you see one, go to an old-established firm. They cannot turn out bad motor-cars, and at the same time be old-established.

POINTS FOR THE OWNER-DRIVER

If you are going to look after the car yourself there are several points to consider when making your purchase.

Motor-cars require most frequent attention in regard to WASHING, POLISHING, OILING, GREASING, BRAKE ADJUSTMENTS, DECARBONIZATION OF ENGINE, VALVE GRINDING, CARBURETTOR, and MAGNETO ADJUSTMENTS.

When going round a car you are examining with a view to purchase, count the number of grease and oil receptacles.

Some cars have a phenomenal number, others are extremely modest in this respect.

Even with the aid of a grease gun, an excellent labour-saving device, lubricating may be a very tiring job, especially if there is an excess of grease nipples.

Examine the position of the grease nipples to see if they are accessible.

Count the number of separate nickle or silvered fittings. They look very pretty, and, in the first pride of ownership, keeping them untarnished may be a labour of love.

Later, one is more inclined to sing a Hymn of Hate.

Black fittings may not be so becoming but they are decidedly more useful.

See that the carburettor and the magneto are easy to get at. Examine the position of the brake adjustment gear. On many modern cars the adjustment of the brakes is an extremely simple matter—as it should be.

Detachable cylinder heads help the business of decarbonizing. Even if you are not going to tackle this job yourself, garages will, or should, charge less for labour if they have not to dismantle the cylinders.

The valves also should be easy to get at.

It is also as well to test the comfort or otherwise of the driving seat, and the position of the various controls. These should be within easy reach of the driver.

If the clutch and accelerator pedals feel awkward when sitting in the car they will feel more awkward during a long journey. If you are of average size you will probably find that the driving seat and controls are suitable.

Most cars, like ready-made suits, are made to a standard size.

In a number of modern cars, however, the driver's seat, the rake of the steering column, the position of the brake and clutch pedals can all be adjusted. If you are tall or short or above the average it is well to seek a car of this type.

For driving comfort you should be able to sit in a natural position, from which position you should be able to reach all the controls without the slightest effort.

THE COST OF MOTORING

Now we come to the most important point of all in regard to the buying of a car.

Do not under any circumstances make up your mind on any particular type of car until you have decided how much you can afford to spend on its upkeep.

Finding the capital to buy a car is often a fairly simple matter; but earning the income to run it is a different proposition.

Many people have *ended* their motoring careers by being too ambitious at the beginning. They have bought big cars and tried to run them on little car incomes. If they had started with little cars they would still be motorists.

The cost of motoring is exaggerated both ways. Owners who have invested in freak cars, or experienced exceptionally bad luck in the matter of repair bills, will tell you that motoring is ruinous. There are others who under-estimate the costs, claiming for their cars an impossible petrol consumption, and an impossible span of life for their tyres.

To arrive at an exact estimate of a year's running costs is, of course, impossible. Luck enters into the problem to a certain degree. If the owner looks after and drives his own car, so much depends on his knowledge of the car.

If he knows sufficient to carry out minor repairs, then his budget will be considerably lessened. The same applies if the owner employs a chauffeur. If he is a good chauffeur he will save his employer a great deal of expense. He will more than earn his salary.

In regard to tyres, there is a large element of luck; but I must say that the modern cord tyres are infinitely more reliable than the old rubber tyre.

Some very remarkable mileage records have already been made with the new cord tyres.

The garage problem has also a big affect on the cost of upkeep. Unfortunately, most of Great Britain was built before the days of motoring, and there are many quite large houses not only without garages, but without any space on which to erect them.

With so many building operations in progress at the present time, designers of houses really should allow in their plans room for the erection of a garage, even in the humbler home.

The day will come, no doubt, when, as in America, every tenth British citizen will possess a motor-car.

The lack of garage accommodation in our big towns is one of the obstacles to the progress of the industry.

If there is room, and he has the means, the intending buyer of a car should build his own garage. It is more satisfactory to have your car close at hand, and it saves money in the long run.

The cost of garaging a car varies. If it is a small car it is often possible to arrange locally for a lock-up at about 7/6 per week.

If it is a big, valuable car, a better home is required, and the figure will be more like £1 a week. A good car deserves a good home.

It is often the case that a man will spend over £1,000—or the pre-war price of a good house—on a motor-car and keep it in a shed which would be more suitable for cattle.

DEPRECIATION

What to allow for depreciation in these days is also a difficult question. If a good car is bought with the intention of keeping it during its lifetime, which should be at least ten years, less than 10 per cent for depreciation need be allowed. The car after ten years will fetch some sort of price.

If it is only intended to keep the car for a few years before making a new purchase, then 20 per cent will have to be allowed for the first year.

A car costing £500 will depreciate probably 20 per cent each year, for the first four years of its life. The really first-class car in the £2,000 class will depreciate only 10 per cent.

A very cheap car might depreciate as much as 45 per cent in the first year.

I do not think depreciation will be so heavy during the next two or three years, as the price of cars is likely to be more or less stable. The present is a very good period for the new motorist. The little tables which I have compiled will provide a guide to motoring costs.

They cover practically every class of car. The expenses are based on a yearly mileage allowance of 7,000. This is about the average yearly mileage of the owner-driver.

Petrol costs are based on the price of No. 1 grade petrol, that is, 2/- a gallon.

The tyre prices are for cord tyres. Rubber tyres are cheaper, but have not the same lasting qualities. No relief from the £1 per h.p. tax can be expected until 1925.

TYPE OF CAR

8 *h.p. Two-seater*

	Running Expenses
Tax, driving licence, and registration -	£8 10 0
Petrol, at 40 miles to the gallon - -	17 10 0
Tyres, allowing 4 new - - -	11 11 0
Oil, 1,000 miles to the gallon - -	5 12 0
Grease - - - - - -	0 12 6
*Insurance, including third-party risks, approx. - - - - - - -	8 5 0
Repairs - - - - - -	5 0 0
Total - - -	£57 0 6

*Insurance based on original cost, £180.

11 h.p. Light Family Car

Tax, driving licence, and registration -	£11	10	0
Petrol, at 35 miles to the gallon - -	20	0	0
Tyres, allowing 4 new - - -	13	9	0
Oil, 1,000 miles to the gallon - -	5	12	0
Grease - - - - - -	0	12	6
*Insurance - - - - - -	12	15	0
Repairs - - - - - -	5	0	0
Total - - -	£68	18	6

*Insurance based on original cost, £255.

12 h.p. Small Family Car

Tax, driving licence, and registration -	£12	10	0
Petrol, at 30 miles to the gallon - -	23	6	0
Tyres, allowing 4 new - - -	20	14	0
Oil, 800 miles to the gallon - -	7	0	0
Grease - - - - - -	0	12	6
*Insurance - - - - - -	12	17	0
Repairs - - - - - -	5	0	0
Total - - -	£81	19	6

*Insurance based on lowest price, £300.

15 h.p. Five-seater

Tax, driving licence, and registration	£15	10	0
Petrol, at 25 miles to the gallon - -	28	0	0
Tyres, allowing 4 new - - -	38	14	0
Oil, 700 miles to the gallon - -	8	0	0
Grease - - - - - -	0	12	6
*Insurance - - - - - -	15	15	0
Repairs - - - - - -	5	0	0
Total - - -	£111	11	6

*Insurance based on lowest price, £350.

20 h.p. Five-seater

Tax, driving licence, and registration -	£20	10	0
Petrol, at 20 miles to the gallon -	35	0	0
Tyres, allowing 4 new - - -	38	14	0
Oil, 600 miles to the gallon - -	9	12	0
Grease - - - - - -	0	12	6
*Insurance - - - - - -	17	15	0
Repairs - - - - - -	5	0	0
Total - - -	**£127**	**3**	**6**

*Insurance based on lowest price; £350.

40 h.p. Car

Tax, driving licence, and registration	£40	10	0
Petrol, at 12 miles to the gallon -	58	6	0
Tyres, allowing 4 new - - -	43	8	0
Oil, 500 miles to the gallon - -	11	4	0
Grease - - - - - -	0	12	6
*Insurance - - - - - -	31	17	3
Repairs - - - - - -	5	0	0
Total - - -	**£190**	**17**	**9**

*Insurance based on lowest price, £1,500.

By the time this table is in print the price of tyres and petrol may have altered, either in an upward or downward direction.

Let us hope in the latter.

The prospective buyer who is considering the type of car most suitable to his purse can easily make his own calculations.

SECOND-HAND CARS

Here advice is rather difficult.

Buying second-hand cars, like buying anything else

second-hand, is a lottery.   Like the curio hunter, you
may pick up a real treasure at a small cost ; on the
other hand, your purchase may be worthless.

As with furniture, flaws can be skilfully camou-
flaged.   There are quite a number of unscrupulous
dealers in the second-hand car market who are
skilled in the faking of cars.

Possibly if one could employ X-rays to examine
the inside of the engine and other vital parts which
are hidden, the task would be simplified.

One thing to beware of is an enamelled engine.
This usually means that there is something to be
concealed—that something being a crack in the
cylinders or the crank-case.

The advertisement columns of the daily news-
papers and the motoring papers form a good medium
for the buyers of second-hand cars, as through them
one can get into touch with the private owner.

Good bargains can be picked up at some of the
auction-rooms.

In some cases the auctioneers give written guaran-
tees with the cars they are selling.

It is a sound plan to buy a second-hand car from
a firm who are agents for that particular make of
car.   It is against their interests, if the car has a
good name in motoring circles, to sell one in a bad
condition.   A bad car, even if it is old and second-
hand, is a bad advertisement for the firm whose
name it bears, and also for the agents who sell it.

Always, when buying a second-hand car, unless
you are yourself an expert, employ an expert to
examine it, and if possible let that expert be a friend.

THE WOMAN DRIVER

I am often asked what is the best type of car
for the woman motorist.   At the time of writing

the army of fair motorists numbers approximately 100,000. May it increase !

Well, from what I have seen of women drivers they require no special make of car. They drive as well as most men, and they have as much mechanical knowledge as many male motorists of to-day.

High-powered cars, especially those with six-cylinder engines, have, owing to their increased docility, become almost safer to drive than some smaller cars. In the old days the sight of a woman driving a 60 h.p. car would have caused admiration, mingled with alarm.

I suppose there are certain considerations which make the modern saloon and coupé especially suitable for the woman driver.

Of this type there is a wide choice, ranging from 10 h.p. upwards.

Many are beautifully furnished, and very pretty to look upon. With the windows wide open on a hot day you can almost get as much fresh air as with an open car, though, of course, you have not the blue sky for your roof.

But you arrive at your destination clean, spotless, and unruffled, which is impossible in an open car, even with the best modern all-weather equipment.

In selecting a closed car the principal point to look for is the window space allowed. For backing, turning, and manœuvring the car generally it is necessary to have a clear all-round view.

From the driver's seat there should be no blind spots. A wide, long window light in the rear part of the car is necessary for backing the car with precision. To the woman buyer I would say, do not be influenced too much by the handsome appearance of a car. Beauty may be a desirable quality, but it is only paint deep. As advertisements frequently tell us, " The soul of a motor-car is its engine."

THE CAR ARRIVES

The great day has arrived. There is a knock at the front door, for which you have been waiting eagerly.

Outside the new treasure stands, dazzling in its virgin freshness, with the engine gently purring over.

It is a great moment, whether you be a hardened old motorist or a recruit to the ranks.

But if this book is to be practical we must not linger too long over the emotions evoked by this happy event. Let us rather suggest some good resolutions which should be made for its future care.

Probably more harm is done by the ill-treatment of a motor-car in its infancy than any other time in its career.

A new motor-car, like a baby, requires special treatment. It is a wise policy to learn at once as much as possible about your new treasure.

In these days manufacturers afford facilities for visiting their works, where it is possible to see the car built. The man who is buying a new car would do well to take advantage of the offer.

He can then see all the interior details, which will be hidden from him in the finished product.

The first thing to ask the man who delivers the car is how far it has been run on its road tests. A new car requires to be run about 500 miles before it settles down, and the engine, gears, springs, and so forth lose their stiffness.

In some cases the makers thoroughly run the car before delivery, but the majority do not.

Therefore, for the first 500 miles it is advisable to travel at a speed of no more than 20 or 25 miles an hour.

On the broad highway this is rather an ordeal. The temptation to let her out in a glorious burst of speed is almost irresistible; but the exercise of restraint under such circumstances may be classed as one of the prime virtues.   The car will thank you for it in later years.

It is one of the worst forms of cruelty to race a new car when its joints are stiff.

KNOW YOUR CAR

As soon as possible after delivery carry out a thorough examination of the new car. Take out the tool-kit and try each spanner, and see what is its particular function. A thorough knowledge of the tools in the kit and their use will save time and trouble later, when jobs have to be tackled on the road. Go round the car with the various spanners. If any of the nuts are too tight on their threads, take them off and give the thread a coat of vaseline or grease. Look out for the painter's trade mark. It may be on the starting handle, on the bonnet catches, or the side curtain fixtures. Remove it with a piece of emery cloth. The slightest blob of paint on a bearing causes an obstruction.

Put the hood up to see how it fits.

Among the preliminary things you should learn about your new car are : How to take out the jet or jets in the carburettor. How to clean the make and break of the magneto. How to put in a new valve spring. How to adjust the brakes. How to change the wheels or rims.

Learn thoroughly the system of oiling and greasing the car. You will probably have a maker's oiling chart explaining the method, but if in doubt get an agent or representative of the firm to show you where and when the car needs oil or grease.

The longest-lived cars are those which receive proper attention in regard to lubrication.

If the doors of the new car are stiff, which is probable, and will not close easily, do not slam them.

Slamming is bad for the paint-work. Undo the catch and exert a steady pressure on the door, when it will probably shut without jarring.

Do not expect the self-starter to work magic.

If you cannot start the car yourself by cranking over with the starting handle, then the self-starter cannot do so.

If the car has been left standing all night, prime the engine as you would if you had to start it yourself, that is, flood the carburettor, close the air shutter, and give the engine a few turns over with the starting handle—keeping the switch off. You will probably find the new engine stiff, but do not be alarmed.

Switch on and press the self-starter push knob. If the engine will not start do some more priming. Only keep the self-starter at work for a few seconds at a time. To run the self-starter continually in the hope that Providence will come to its aid is hopeless ; meanwhile the battery is suffering. The melody of a self-starter grinding away hopelessly for minutes on end is distressing music.

EASY STARTING

The following is the correct and easiest method of starting most cars when they have been at rest for sometime :—

Flood the carburettor. Close the air shutter. If there is no automatic method of doing this, stuff the air shutter up with rag. Switch the engine off. Crank the engine over half a dozen times by hand, then switch on and start with the self-starter.

Let the engine run for a short period, then open the air shutter. On cold days easy starting may be assisted by filling the radiator with hot water, and introducing a few drops of petrol into the cylinders through the plugs or compression caps.

LEARNING TO DRIVE

I am not going to take my readers through the mechanical motions of driving. A day on the road with an experienced driver will teach more about the purely technical side of driving than a whole book of words and illustrations.

But the operations of declutching, gear changing, steering, and so forth, are only a small part of the art of good driving—and good driving *is* an art. These operations are really very simple ; in fact, a case was known of a man who had never been in a motor-car before, and who, without any previous instructions, except of a verbal nature, drove a car from London to Brighton.

But in the very fact that driving a car is simple lies the danger. If driving is simple, safe driving is certainly not.

It is worth while for your own safety, and for your own satisfaction, to become a skilled driver. There are, sad to say, only a few expert drivers on the road. Recent figures published by the Ministry of Transport show that over 80 per cent. of motor-car accidents are due to bad driving. The following are some important driving DO'S and DON'TS :—

Do not learn to drive on your new car. Do not start down an unknown hill at speed.

Give way whenever possible to the man who is driving uphill. If you block his way you may spoil one of the motorist's most pleasant thrills, that is, a good top-gear hill climb.

Do not pass any vehicle on the road unless you can see beyond a peradventure that the road ahead is clear.

Never pass another car going in your direction on a bend of the road.

On a steep and unknown hill change down to lower gear. The lower gear will act as an additional brake.

When coming out of a by-road on to a main road *Stop*, *Look*, and *Listen*. Risks taken here are the biggest cause of road accidents. The man on the main road has the right of way, and is very jealous of this right. To dispute this right often leads to disaster. At the subsequent inquest the jury will find that the man who came out of the side turning was to blame.

It may sound uncomplimentary, but, when driving, look on all other drivers as fools.

When you meet a fool—there are plenty on the road—you will then be ready for him.

In the old days, whenever a motorist observed another motorist in trouble on the road he stopped to offer assistance. Help to revive this old-time chivalry.

There are certain small up and down hills mostly running over rivers and culverts, which completely obscure the view of the road ahead.

Treat these hills as blind corners, that is, approach them slowly and carefully and sound your horn.

Allow fast vehicles to overtake you. Overtake other vehicles on the right or off side.

Never overtake at cross-roads, bends in the road, or down steep hills.

Tramway cars in most towns can be passed on either near or off side. It is best to pass on the off side a stationary tram-car which will, when it starts, travel in your direction. Exercise caution when passing tramway cars as their passengers are apt to jump off without looking.

Stop at once when asked to do so by the police, or when involved in any mishap, even though it be a minor one.

Observe all official warning posts and signs and the directions of the police.

When driving in towns always pass road standards on your left side.

THE POLICE

On the whole, the police are a courteous body of men. They have to administer the law, even if in regard to speed limits on the open road " it is an ass." But this is not the policeman's fault.

In a long career of motoring, I have always found the police considerate, helpful, and possessed of more than an ordinary share of common sense. To abuse a policeman who is carrying out the letter of the law is unfair and foolish.

A reasonable explanation is often accepted by the common-sense policeman when a trivial infringement of a trivial by-law is concerned. But abuse very naturally does not encourage the policeman to draw on his normal fund of common sense.

If you are caught breaking the law, save up for the magistrate your views of the absurdity of that particular law.

SKILLED DRIVING SAVES WEAR AND TEAR

The following DO's and DON'Ts are part of the mechanical side of driving. If observed, they will add to the longevity of the car :—

On a long journey do not drive with your foot continually on the clutch pedal. When on the alert in traffic this is necessary, but on the open road it is not necessary and is unadvisable. You are probably quite unconsciously placing a tension on the clutch operating gear. The result of this is often seen in a slipping clutch.

Never turn the steering wheel when the car is stationary. This is a very common mistake. It is mostly done in garages, in order to straighten up the front wheels preliminary to taking the car out.

It throws a tremendous strain on the steering gear.

The car has gears in order to relieve the engine when it is put under a strain; therefore always change gear when the engine shows the slightest sign of distress. It is not a sign of good driving to take a stiff hill on top gear with the engine knocking and spluttering in distress. There is no glory in such a climb.

If you are good at judging distances there should be little necessity for using the brakes. The brakes are there really for emergencies. To the bad motorist these emergencies occur every few minutes. Every time you use the brakes you are taking some of the fabric off your tyres.

On long hills use the hand and foot brakes alternately.

When driving in traffic, slipping the clutch often saves changing gear, but neither the clutch nor the engine likes it.

RECOGNIZED ROAD SIGNALS

The following are the recognized driving signals, which should be observed by all drivers under all circumstances :—

About to Stop.—Right forearm held up vertically, with hand outstretched.

Turning to the Right.—Right arm held out parallel with the ground, hand outstretched.

Turning to the Left.—Right arm held out in a line with the shoulder and swept to the left in the direction of the left hand turning.

Slowing Down; Danger Ahead.—Quick up and down motion of the right hand held outside the car.

You can Pass Me.—Right arm held outside the car and swept forward with the motion of under-hand bowling at cricket.

While these signals are a safeguard if properly given, their misuse is equally dangerous.

The mere act of giving a signal will not stop a car.

For instance, if you are going to turn to the right it is no good extending your right arm and turning the car simultaneously.

As far as the man who is following is concerned, you might just as well not have given the signal at all.

All warning signals should be given in plenty of time, and should not be acted upon until the person for whom they are intended has had time to see them, and to take his own precautions.

Always give the signals clearly and correctly.

At the same time, if you yourself are in the position of the following car, and are not clear as to the meaning of the signals given by the driver ahead, slow down or stop until it is perfectly clear what the giver of the signals intends to do.

In fact, the following is always a good motoring motto : " When in Doubt Slow Down."

The " Please Pass Me " signal should always be given to the driver of a following car who blows his horn for a right of way. If you give this signal, he knows beyond a doubt that it is safe for him to pass.

If you do not give it he is in doubt as to whether you have heard his horn, and for all he knows you may pull over to the right hand side of the road just as he is passing you.

Do not pass a car on a narrow road until you yourself get the passing signal.

PREVENTION OF SKIDDING

With the very clever anti-skid designs in the treads of modern cord and rubber tyres the danger of bad skids has been greatly reduced.

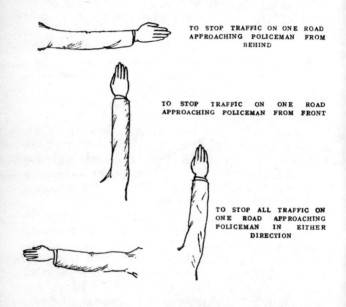

TO STOP TRAFFIC ON ONE ROAD APPROACHING POLICEMAN FROM BEHIND

TO STOP TRAFFIC ON ONE ROAD APPROACHING POLICEMAN FROM FRONT

TO STOP ALL TRAFFIC ON ONE ROAD APPROACHING POLICEMAN IN EITHER DIRECTION

POINT POLICEMAN'S SIGNALS WHICH WERE RECENTLY ADOPTED AS STANDARD SIGNALS FOR THE POLICE IN ALL PARTS OF THE COUNTRY

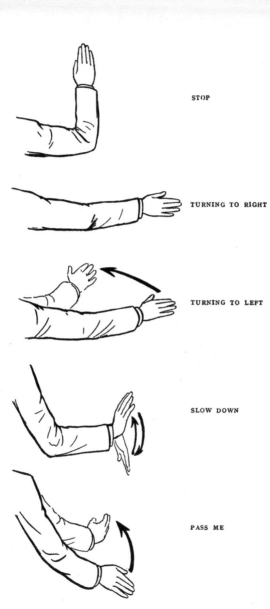

STOP

TURNING TO RIGHT

TURNING TO LEFT

SLOW DOWN

PASS ME

Even so, skidding is still a real danger, and is apt to inspire the beginner with terror.

Prevention is better than cure.

The skilful—that is, the careful—driver is very rarely forced into a position where skidding is necessary.

There are several kinds of skids.

Let us first take the skid which occurs on a wet road. The roads with wood surfaces are usually most dangerous in this respect.

In nearly every case the skid is caused by the sudden application of the brakes. This means that the driver has misjudged his distance. It is an extraordinary thing how motor-cars, like sheep, herd together. Go out on any of the main roads at week-ends and you will find little flocks of motor-cars, led probably by a big one, with long gaps between the flocks.

There is really no need to follow on the heels of the car in front. Either pass the car ahead or keep a reasonable distance from it, in which case, if he has to pull up, you have plenty of space in which to slow down.

A skid is one of the most sudden things that happens to a motorist. An emergency arises when it is necessary to put on the brakes, and the instant this happens the back of the car swings round. When a bad skid occurs the car may make a complete turn, and the driver will find himself travelling in the opposite direction.

As the skid is sudden, it necessitates very quick correction. There is no time for meditation.

The most natural action for the beginner is to jam on his brakes still harder, in order to check the erratic behaviour of the car.

This only increases the trouble. The best way to correct a back wheel skid on a wet road is :

(1) Declutch.

(2) Steer in the direction in which the rear of the car is trying to go.

If the back of the car is sliding to the left, turn the steering wheel to the left.

The clutch may now be let in gently, and the car should pull straight on the road again.

In addition to the sudden application of the brakes there are other causes for side-slip on a wet road :

Sudden acceleration, sudden divergence from the straight path, taking a turn too quickly, and letting in the clutch fiercely.

One of the most dangerous forms of skidding, which fortunately very rarely occurs, is a front wheel skid. The driver turns the wheel to pass a vehicle on a wet road and the car does not respond, but carries on in a straight line.

The only method for the correction of a front wheel skid is to create a back wheel skid, that is, apply the brakes suddenly.

Then correct the back wheel skid.

In these days of tarred roads a dry skid is a rare occurrence, but such skids do occur on roads on which the cambered sides are steep.

Such skids are assisted by tyres which have seen long service, and have lost their non-skid thread.

Some motorists are apt to boast about the longevity of their tyres, but it is as well, once the non-skid thread has worn away, to give up boasting and buy new ones. Worn tyres have led to several fatal accidents in recent times. The best cure for a dry skid on a heavily cambered road is prevention.

Keep off the camber and never pass another car if it necessitates getting on to the cambered sides of the road.

THE HOLIDAY TOUR

We have been pottering about with a new car for some little time. We have essayed a successful week-end trip or two, and have whetted our appetites for adventures further afield. In fact we are now looking forward to the holiday tour. The call of the " open road," the much used but pleasantly sounding phrase, is irresistible.

We take out our maps and unfold them. What a choice is before us ! We have done with mere sections ; now we want the whole length and breadth of Britain. Radiating from, let us say, London as a centre are red lines—hundreds and hundreds of them—intersecting the green, and running over hill and dale, through tiny hamlets and great towns, finding their way across the borders of Scotland and Wales, wending their way with the rivers, and doing their best to keep in touch with the coastline of the four seas. These are the roads to joy and happiness.

It is a wonderful choice, and the mapping out of the programme holds in it a fascination of anticipation.

The success or otherwise of a tour is largely dependent on our preliminary arrangements. In the first place, the car must be in tip-top order. Do not leave anything to luck.

If the car is a new one it will naturally need little attention, but if we have been running it all the winter then we should carry out a minor overhaul.

Small faults which were not troublesome on the short runs may develop into real evils when the car is called on to put forth its best efforts day after day.

The engine should be free from all carbon. There should be no leakage of compression at the valve caps or sparking plugs.

The brakes should be in proper adjustment. This

is of vital importance, especially if the owner lives in a town where his pottering about is done on flat roads.

Brakes which are quite efficient in, say, Essex, may be thoroughly dangerous in Devon, Cornwall, the Peak district, and so forth. The tyres should receive careful attention. Tyres which have stood up to hard work on short runs are apt to collapse on long journeys.

There is nothing so tragic as continuous tyre trouble when on tour. Old tyres should be replaced by new.

The wheels should be taken off, the tyres closely examined, and all flints which have become lodged in the rubber should be extracted.

If in the course of extraction big holes are left in the rubber or cord fabric these should be vulcanized.

The whole car should receive before the start a thorough oiling and greasing, as per oiling instruction chart supplied by the makers.

There is a great sense of satisfaction in starting off on the great morning with a car in its very fittest condition. All preliminary arrangements in regard to this are well repaid.

THE DAILY PROGRAMME

I really believe that many carefully planned tours which might otherwise have proved successful are spoiled by a too-ambitious programme in regard to the daily mileage. Some holiday programmes look far too much like work, and, after all, a motoring tour is usually intended to be a holiday.

The beginner generally allows for too high an average speed.

From a long experience of touring in Britain and abroad I should say that an average speed of 20 miles per hour is a sound allowance.

This gives you time to make up any leeway caused by minor mishaps on the road, and these will happen even with the best regulated cars.

It also allows you and your passengers to see something of the countryside.

It is well to remember if you are driving that your passengers have not the same interest as you in high speed.

Bursts of speed on good roads are exhilarating, but if you arrange your programme on a 30 miles per hour basis it means high speed all the way. In the event of a stoppage on the road it means a race to make up time.

It often leads to loss of dinner, loss of temper, and fatigue, which means loss of enjoyment. If you average 20 miles per hour and drive for six hours a day, which is well under trade union hours, this will give you a total mileage of 120.

Supposing in a week you allow three days off for sightseeing, exercise which is very necessary for motoring, and your allied hobbies such as photography, then you have a weekly mileage of 600. In a three weeks' tour you can cover in comfort and without fatigue 1,800 miles, which will take you the length and breadth of Britain.

This is a very sound basis on which to work out your plans. The biggest ' DON'T ' in connection with touring is DON'T overdo it.

THE ROUTE

I am not going to suggest any particular part of Britain as a touring ground. Personally, I love all of it. It is only when you get in a car and explore the countryside that you realize how really beautiful Britain is.

Good roads are essential to comfortable touring, and it is as well to make inquiries from your Motoring Association before planning your route.

Remember that a road which has a nice fat red line across the map indicates only that it is a first-class road. The map-makers do not guarantee in these days that it is a good road.

In some cases the by-ways are in better condition than the highways, and pass through much more interesting country.

But whether you choose the highways or by-ways, find out their condition beforehand.

The roads of Britain are undergoing great changes. Whole stretches of the big main roads are being widened and straightened, and some of these for mile after mile are under repair. The best maps to work on, in my mind, are the new shilling ordnance maps issued by the Ministry of Transport, which are thoroughly up to date in regard to all the new roads. So far twenty-nine sections of these maps have been issued, covering England and Wales.

These maps give all the first- and second-class roads, with the numbers allotted to them, following completion by the Ministry of Transport of the classification of British roads.

All the first- and second-class roads now have their official numbers. These numbers have not such a romantic flavour about them as the old names to which we have been accustomed, but the numbers certainly help you to find your way about the country.

The Great North Road, for example, is now known as A.1 throughout its length.

A.1 appears on the sign-boards, and as long as you see this on the boards you know you are travelling in the right direction. There is no need to examine the sign-boards for the names of the intermediate towns.

3

SPARES ON TOUR

Always keep the spare tyre in good condition. If a puncture occurs and the spare tyre has to be used, take the first opportunity of mending it.

Always carry a reserve of petrol. If the spare tank or can has to be used, refill it at the earliest opportunity.

Have a full tool-kit.

An electric torch is invaluable if you are going to do any night travelling. Night repairs or adjustments are an abomination in the dark.

Spare sparking plugs, lamp bulbs, valve springs, and an assortment of nuts should also be taken.

Possibly the most valuable spares of all are a sheet of emery paper, a piece of insulating tape, and some copper wire. With these you can work miracles in the way of temporary repairs. Insulating tape will seal up leaks, emery will smooth obstinate fittings, and copper wire will tie up most things securely.

These should form the motorist's first-aid outfit. A length of fuse wire is also useful.

PICNICKING

The invention of domestic labour-saving devices has made picnicking on the road worth while. Bad catering on the part of many hotels is also an encouragement to take our meals in Nature's surroundings. A motor picnic need no longer consist of sandwiches hastily consumed by the roadside. All kinds of clever devices have been invented for the benefit of motor tourists. Stainless knives, forks, spoons, and even plates help washing-up—always an unpleasant aftermath of any meal.

The lightness of modern aluminium camp-fire

fittings allows them to be carried easily. Collapsible aluminium drinking flasks can be compressed into a very small space. In fact the whole paraphernalia for a four-course dinner can be carried in a well-designed and compact little picnic basket.

For our cooking we can carry solidified petrol, the old soldiers' friend, on which Tommy cooked his meals in the trenches. Thermos flasks are now very cheap and efficient, and can be used not only for carrying tea, but also for hot soup.

But modern inventions carry us even further. There can now be bought a complete fireless cooker, which will not only keep your food hot all day, but, if desired, will actually cook it on the journey.

It consists of a container inside which are fitted three iron plates. These iron plates are heated before we start on our journey and slipped into the container. The food to be cooked is then placed in the container.

It is not merely a question of stews and ragouts, but the container will actually roast joints, fowls, and so forth. These containers can be bought from the principal camp equipment dealers.

This style of cooker was recently used at one of the King's shooting parties, and on this occasion pheasants were roasted in the container during a forty miles' journey from the shooting-box.

No basting is necessary, as the joint or bird cooks itself and retains all its juices.

It will be seen that by obtaining proper equipment very desirable meals can be served up—and the motorist when touring needs good nourishment.

The motorist in a hurry resents any time lost on the road.

He is satisfied with a sandwich lunch, but I do not think he enjoys himself as much as the more leisurely motorist.

Choosing a good spot for the meal is important. It is unwise to fix on any definite time.

If you arrange for lunch at 1 p.m. you may at that particular time be in uncongenial surroundings. The best policy is to allow half an hour for the pleasant occupation of Looking for a Good Picnic site.

The requirements are : a sunny spot if it is a cool day, a shady spot if it is a hot day, shelter from the wind, pretty surroundings, a neighbouring pool to do any washing-up that is necessary, and a place where the car can be parked off the road.

The car itself is an asset, as the running boards can be used as sideboards.

DASHBOARD DELIGHTS

There is something very fascinating about a well-equipped dashboard. There was a time when practically the whole of the dashboard fittings were classed by motor manufacturers as accessories.

It was by no means unusual to have to pay as much as £100 for accessories before the car was fit to take out on the road.

Nowadays manufacturers have learned wisdom, and the modern equipment of a motor-car is usually sufficient.

For ordinary driving one should have on the dashboard, apart from the ordinary switches, a speedometer, an oil indicator, and a dash-light.

These are necessities, but there are other extras with which you can experiment, and which add greatly to the interest of driving.

The instruments I mention below can all be obtained from accessory dealers. There is a petrol meter which will tell you the amount of petrol your car is consuming. This provides a constant source of interest and is an aid to intelligent driving. You can, for instance, tell by its readings the most economical speed for your car, and you can regulate your jet openings accordingly. An aid to correct gear changing is an engine revolution meter which tells you, when your car is on the move, the speed of your engine revolutions.

By watching the meter at work and discovering the correct revolutions for a change down you can make the operation of gear changing standard. In wet weather one of the chief annoyances to the driver is an obscured wind-screen.

There are highly efficient automatic wind-screen wipers on the market. I think the best kinds are those which are worked by the suction of the engine.

In this case the power used for the wind-screen wiper costs nothing.

A dashboard meter which shows the gradient of the hills is also a source of great interest, especially when touring in Devonshire, the Peak district, and other hilly places.

It is not of course an essential, but it is none the less an interesting gadget.

For night driving a spot light, that is, a lamp which can be swivelled in any direction by the driver, is invaluable. The best form of spot light is one that is independent of the battery which supplies the ordinary lamps. If the main battery fails, the spot light can be used as an emergency lamp. It is useful as an anti-dazzle light, for it can be so fixed that its beam comes below the vision of the drivers of approaching traffic.

In fog, which is as much a terror to the motorist as to the sea pilot, the spot light can be so fixed as to illuminate the edge of the road. A dashboard plug indicator is another new luxury. This will show at a glance any failure on the part of the sparking plugs, and will also tell you in which cylinder the faulty plug is located.

Add to this a thermometer, which tells you the temperature of the water in the radiator, and you have a fair knowledge of the engine's secrets without opening the bonnet.

I do not for the moment recommend that the owner of a little 8 h.p. car should burden it with all these gadgets ; in fact you would not have room on the dashboard for half of them ; but I find that many motorists are interested in these extras, and those I have mentioned I have personally tested and found efficient.

SOME PARTS OF A CAR EXPLAINED

The Engine.—In order to be able to correct minor faults it is as well to have some knowledge, even if elementary, of how the engine works.

It is curious, but none the less true, that there are thousands of motor-car owners on the road who have not the faintest idea why their car goes.

As a matter of fact, a motor-car engine is really a very simple piece of mechanism. The force which moves a motor-car is an explosion, or a series of explosions. The principle is the same in all motor-car engines, whether two-stroke, four-stroke, or of the sleeve-valve design. The explosion is caused by igniting petrol gases under compression.

This is what is happening all the time in your engine. The petrol is either forced by pressure or arrives on its own account propelled by the laws of gravity from the petrol tank, through a pipe to the carburettor. It arrives first of all in the float chamber. Thence the petrol, the supply of which is regulated by the float, now passes through a jet. It is joined by a correct proportion of air, which may be regulated automatically or can be controlled from the dashboard.

The jet breaks up the petrol into very small particles, which are sprayed into the combustion chamber.

It is now in a fit condition to vaporize. It is the petrol vapour which is shortly going to be exploded.

For the purpose of this description we will take an ordinary four-cylinder four-stroke water-cooled engine. Inside the cylinders are four pistons. These pistons are connected by connecting rods to a crank-shaft. Inside the cylinder the following events happen : (1) Let us call it the suction stroke. The piston descends the cylinder sucking the petrol vapour through what is called the inlet valve, which is now open. (2) Compression stroke. The piston ascends the cylinder and compresses the petrol vapour. During this proceeding the inlet valve and the exhaust valve are closed.

(3) Explosion stroke.—Everything is now ready for the sparking plug to do its work. When the piston has got to the top of its stroke and is on the point of descending, a spark appears at the point of the plug, explodes the petrol mixture, and sends the piston with great force down the cylinder. This turns the crank-shaft, which turns the fly-wheel, which turns the clutch when engaged, which turns the gear wheels, which turns the propeller-shaft, which ultimately turns the back wheels.

(4) Exhaust stroke.—The piston comes up the cylinder, but this time the exhaust valve is open and the exploded gases are forced out through this valve opening. This cycle of events is going on in each cylinder alternately and at a tremendous speed.

The Crank-shaft.—The piston inside the cylinders is connected to the crank-shaft by means of a connecting rod. The connexions between the piston, the connecting rod, and the crank-shaft form important bearings.

Bridging the piston is what is called a gudgeon pin. The end of the connecting rod which fits on to the gudgeon pin is called the SMALL END. The end which is connected with the crank-shaft is called the BIG END.

The crank-shaft itself rests on main bearings. When the explosion occurs inside the cylinders it forces down the piston and the connecting rod which turns the crank-shaft. After a time the small and big end bearings need testing for " play," that is, looseness.

Taking up these bearings is a job that should not be attempted by the amateur.

The Cam-shaft.—This shaft operates the valves. On it are cams which at the correct time strike the tappets which lift the valves. It is usually driven by a gear wheel from the crank-shaft.

The Fly-wheel is a big wheel aft of the engine, which balances the crank-shaft and forms a housing for the clutch.

The Clutch.—This allows the car to start from rest without shock. It also allows the engine to run free when the car is at rest. It transmits the power of the engine to the gear box and enables the gears to be changed without difficulty.

There are many types of clutch, the most usual being the leather cone or plate type. Plate clutches require little attention ; leather clutches need an occasional dressing of collan oil.

The Propellor-shaft.—This transmits the power from the gear box to the rear axle.

Universal Joints.—One joins the propeller-shaft to the gear box, the other to the rear axle. Some modern joints are made of fabric, which need occasional dressing of salad or collan oil.

The Differential.—It would give both you and myself a headache to describe the workings of the differential. Neither is it necessary, as the modern differential rarely causes trouble. Briefly, it is an arrangement of gear wheels in the back axle which enables one road wheel when corners are taken to travel more slowly than the others. This gives comfortable riding round corners, saves strain on the driving mechanism and wear and tear of tyres.

ROAD TROUBLES

Having grasped the elementary principles of the working of our engine we are in a better position to put matters right when troubles occur on the road.

When our car comes to a sudden stop for the first time we are apt to be a little bewildered.

The thousand and one ills that we have read about in our textbooks flash before our minds in bewildering array.

But unless something very serious has happened, which with the modern car is very rare, we shall be able to arrive at the seat of the trouble very quickly by the process of elimination.

In 90 cases out of 100 the trouble will be due to either of two main causes.

The engine is not getting its petrol mixture, or the petrol mixture is not being exploded—that is, the sparking plugs are not firing.

The first thing is to see if the petrol is getting as far as the carburettor. This can easily be tested by seeing if the float chamber will fill. If the carburettor floods in the ordinary way, I should then test the ignition.

Take a screwdriver with a wooden handle and connect the metal part of the screwdriver to the terminal of the plug, placing the edge of the screwdriver a fraction of an inch away from the cylinder head.

Then press the self-starter, or get someone to turn over the engine by hand.

If the plug is firing a spark should occur at the

point of the contact between the screwdriver end and the cylinder head.

If no assistance is available for this test, and it is not possible to press the self-starter button and hold the screwdriver at the same time, the test can be carried out by unscrewing a plug and laying it on the top of the cylinder, taking care that the terminals or sparking points are not in contact with the cylinder head.

The engine can then be turned by hand, and, if the ignition is in order, a spark should appear.

If it does not, then we know, at any rate, the cause of the trouble. If the engine stopped suddenly, it probably means that the ignition system itself is at fault and not individual plugs.

The engine will run, though badly, with two or even one cylinder firing.

If the sparking plugs are firing properly, then we must return to the carburettor. So far an examination has only been made of the float chamber. Let us now see if the petrol is passing from the float chamber into and through the jet. Possibly the jet will be found to be choked. The jet aperture is a very tiny hole, only a fraction of an inch in circumference.

If this hole becomes choked, it is a very small happening, but it has very big results. It brings the whole of the car to a stop.

It is no use here in describing the various ways of taking out a jet or jets. There are a wide variety of carburettors, each one having a different method of fitting the jet.

That is why in an earlier section of this book the reader was recommended to learn exactly how to extract the jet when taking over his new car. The obstruction in the jet can be moved as a rule by blowing through the jet, or if the obstruction is fixed in the aperture of the jet may be removed with a pin.

It is sometimes possible to locate jet troubles by the behaviour of the engine. If the ignition gives out then the engine will stop at once. But with a choked jet there is often a sighing and spluttering before the engine comes to rest.

When this spluttering begins it is occasionally possible to dislodge the obstruction by accelerating the engine suddenly and letting it race for a few seconds.

Another possible cause of carburettor trouble may be a leak in the pipe which leads from the petrol tank to the carburettor. This will, of course, be at once obvious.

It is also as well before starting to dismantle the jet, to make sure that there is petrol in the tank.

We will now turn to the ignition. We will take it that none of the plugs are firing. An examination must now be made of the magneto.

Most beginners in motoring are very much frightened of a magneto.

They really need not be, as it is a very simple piece of mechanism, as far as minor adjustments are concerned. But, again, if the owner-driver is going to tackle his minor adjustments, he must learn where the seat of trouble is likely to be found.

He should know where the contact breaker is and how to dismantle it. This is the part of the magneto where trouble usually occurs. The position of the collector and distributor brushes and how to dismantle them should also be known.

The first possibility is that the earth wire leading to the switch may have come adrift or broken, causing a short circuit. To test for this, remove the contact breaker cover, and see if the engine will start. If it does the cause of the trouble has been located. The switch is at fault.

The removal of the cover disconnects the switch,

and the journey can now be continued and the switch repaired at the nearest garage, or by yourself at home.

If, however, the removal of the cover has no results, we must next examine the contact breaker.

Get someone to turn the engine over slowly, while you yourself watch the platinum points to see if they are opening and closing.

It may be found that they either remain open or closed. A stuck contact breaker usually means that the operating mechanism needs cleaning; hence the importance of knowing how to dismantle this part of the magneto.

If the points of the contact breaker are opening and closing it is possible that they may be dirty. They should be cleaned with a piece of glass paper.

If the trouble is not yet located, then the collector and distributor brushes, which, as their name suggests, pick up and distribute the current, must be examined.

Possibly the source of trouble here may be a hole in the insulating fabric through which the current is going to waste.

A temporary repair can be made by filling the hole with sealing wax, and binding it with insulating tape. The brushes which are of carbon are carried on springs. They may possibly have become stuck in their holders; in this case a little petrol will probably ease them.

If either brush is broken a temporary repair can be made by trueing up the end of the brush, and extending the spring to make up for the length of brush which has broken away.

An idle day in the garage spent in examining and dismantling the above-mentioned parts will help you in carrying out any repairs necessary on the road.

DECARBONIZATION

To keep an engine fit certain jobs have to be carried out at intervals. One of these is decarbonization. This is a task that can be done by the amateur with a very appreciable saving to his pocket. An ordinary well-behaved engine should not require attention in this respect until it has run for about 5,000 miles. An air-cooled engine may need decarbonizing after 2,000 miles. With detachable cylinder heads the job is a very simple one. Care must, however, be taken to obtain a proper air-tight joint when the head is replaced. Use the same material for the joint as that used by the makers of the engine.

When there is no detachable head, the cylinders will have to be removed.

The best method of learning the process is, of course, to see it done.

A carbonized engine means that a hard carbon deposit has formed on the top of the pistons, in the combustion chamber, and possibly round the piston ring grooves.

This naturally effects the compression space inside the cylinder ; also the deposit becoming white-hot with the heat generated in the cylinders is apt to usurp the function of the sparking plugs.

It causes the explosive mixture to explode before its time.

Symptoms which will indicate that the engine is suffering from carbonization are : knocking unduly when the ignition is advanced, pre-ignition, over-heating, and loss of power on hills.

To take off the cylinders, the carburettor, the exhaust and ignition pipes, oil and petrol pipes, and various controls must be removed.

The beginner should note very carefully the position of all nuts and screws.

While the removal of the cylinders is a comparatively simple task, replacing them may present a difficult problem unless care has been taken to observe the correct fitting of the various accessories.

To prevent confusion replace as soon as possible all nuts on their correct bolts, and all screws on their threads.

Having removed the accessories of the engine, the nuts bolting the cylinders to the crank-case can now be slackened off.

The cylinders must be lifted carefully from their base. They should be lifted with a backward and forward motion. With an engine of any size assistance will probably be required.

When they are removed fill the inside of the cylinders and the pistons with clean rags to prevent dirt getting in ; also cover over the exposed crank-case with waste material.

The carbon deposit will now be visible on the top of the pistons and round the piston ring grooves and in the combustion chamber.

It is as well to remove the piston rings, but care must be taken, as they are made of brittle metal.

This metal is of a springy nature and the rings can be expanded and taken from their grooves and slid over the top of the piston.

The bottom ring should be removed first and replaced first.

A good knife with a sharp point, or a screwdriver with a keen edge, are the best implements for removing the carbon.

Patience is required, but if the job is done thoroughly your efforts are well repaid.

When all trace of carbon deposit has been removed from the top of the piston, the grooves, and the combustion chamber, clean up with a rag dipped in paraffin, or, better still, a stiff brush.

When fitting the piston rings back in their grooves

see that the slight openings where the ends of the piston rings meet do not come together. If they do it will mean loss of compression. In refitting the cylinders—help will again be needed—get them into position at the top of the piston, then squeeze the piston rings together and slide the cylinder down over them. The cylinders can now be bolted to the crank-case.

When tightening the nuts at the base of the cylinders, exert an even tightening pressure on each nut.

In other words, do not tighten up one nut and then turn to the next. Give each in succession a half turn with the spanner until they are all tight.

Even with a detachable cylinder head, it is as well occasionally to remove the complete cylinder, as if the detachable head only is removed it is not possible to get at the piston rings.

There is on the market a chemical for removing carbon which simplifies the job.

The chemical is introduced into the cylinder, through the sparking plug and valve cap openings. As a temporary expedient I have found this chemical very efficient.

By using it the job of hand decarbonizing can be delayed to a large extent without any bad effects on the engine.

VALVE GRINDING

Another job the owner-driver should be able to attend to himself is that of grinding-in the valves. We have already described the function of the valves —the inlet valve, allowing the petrol mixture to pass into the combustion chamber ; and the exhaust valve, allowing the exploded gases to pass out.

On the compression stroke both valves are closed. They should form, when down on their seatings, an airtight bearing.

NEW MINISTRY OF TRANSPORT ROAD DANGER SIGNS

LEVEL CROSSING

STEEP HILL

CORNER

DOUBLE CORNER

NEW MINISTRY OF TRANSPORT ROAD DANGER SIGNS

Loss of compression is one sign that the valves need grinding-in. The compression can be tested by turning over the engine with the starting handle.

If there is a loss of compression the engine will turn over more easily than normally. It will probably be found that one or two cylinders have weak compression.

In this case it is as well to grind-in all the valves.

Valve grinding is made far more easy if the proper tools are used. It is as well, if you intend to tackle this job yourself, to buy (1) A valve lifting tool. (2) A valve grinding tool.

Also required are a screwdriver, fine emery mixed with water or oil, or a mixture of emery and graphite. Special mixtures can be bought of accessory dealers.

By using a mechanical lifter the valve can be easily lifted from its seating, and the key which holds it in position can be withdrawn without difficulty.

The valve is now free to be lifted out.

Remove the valve cap or sparking plug. Insert the edge of a screwdriver into the slot at the top of the valve, and, exerting a sideways pressure, work the valve out of its seating. In the case of an obstinate valve turn the engine until the valve is lifted off its seating. Then take a piece of wire, make a noose in it, and drop it round the neck of the valve, and pull.

Now examine the face of the valve. If it is badly pitted and worn it will probably have to be trued up on a lathe.

This job should not be attempted by the amateur unless he has a good knowledge of the working of a lathe. He may ruin the valve and the lathe too.

He should send the valve to a garage. But valves should not get in this condition unless they have been badly neglected.

Grinding-in a valve by hand is simple, but needs patience. A thin coating of emery mixture should be rubbed on the face of the valve.

The valve is then placed on its seating and the valve grinding instrument is brought into operation. An ordinary screwdriver can be used but it is a tiring process.

The valve is now twisted backwards and forwards with a right and left rotary movement. The valve should be taken out every now and then to see how the work is progressing.

When there is a bright, even, uninterrupted line round the face of the valve you will know that it is properly down on its seating and that no leakage can take place.

After grinding, carefully remove all the emery mixture both from the valve face and the valve seating.

It is possible that, after grinding, the tappet adjustment may not be accurate owing to the fact that the valve has been let down slightly on its seating.

This should be tested and if necessary corrected.

The tappet is the mechanism which lifts the valve. On most modern cars the tappets are adjustable.

When the valve is closed, that is, when it is down on its seating, the tappet should just clear the valve by the thickness of a visiting card.

Do not expect immediate results from your valve grinding. Give the engine a run of 50 miles or so to enable the valves to settle down, then test whether you have done the job properly by taking the car out on to your favourite test hill.

IS YOUR CAR FIT?

It is often difficult to detect in ordinary running whether a motor-car engine is up to its proper standard of efficiency.

The simplest way of testing whether your car is up to the mark is to have a trial hill of your own.

Though a steep hill, it need not be a freak hill.

There should be a hill of this sort within easy reach of your home.

The best type of hill is one which has well-defined landmarks dotted at intervals on the gradient.

My own test hill (I will not reveal its identity or it will no longer be mine) has four landmarks.

The foot of the hill is the steepest part. About 50 yards up is a lamp-post ; beyond this the road takes a sharp turn, and here the gradient is not so steep.

Just past the bend is my second landmark—a pillar-box. Before reaching the top there are two other features which I use—an ancient oak-tree and a telegraph pole.

These landmarks are important as they assist you in arriving at a formula on which you can base your test.

When my car is running at its best it will carry me as far as the lamp-post without a change of gear.

I have to come down to second to negotiate the bend, but at the pillar-box I can again get into top gear without placing too great a strain on the engine. By the time I reach the oak-tree I have to change down to second again, but if the car is running well I can again get into top gear when reaching the telegraph pole.

In order to arrive at a proper formula for your test it is necessary to take the car up the test hill when it is at its best.

It is as well to make a note of its behaviour under these conditions.

Your " Log " should read something after this wise :

Started at foot of hill at 20 miles per hour with ignition fully advanced.

Changed gear when level with lamp-post. Changed up again at pillar-box.

Between pillar-box and oak-tree car reached maximum speed of 30 miles per hour.

Changed down at oak-tree.

Between oak-tree and telegraph pole car reached maximum speed of 25 miles per hour.

Changed up at telegraph pole.

No knock of engine at any point of hill with ignition fully advanced.

These landmarks are, of course, fictitious. You will have to find similar landmarks of your own.

Any other points worthy of notice in the running of the car should be entered in the " Log." It is far better to have this written down in your motoring diary, as one's memory in motoring matters is apt to be treacherous.

You can now use this " Log " in connexion with all future tests. If you suspect that your car is ailing, take it out to the test hill. You must choose a time when the hill is free from any impediment in the way of other traffic. Endeavour to drive the car in exactly the same way as you did in your standard test, that is, start at the bottom at 20 miles per hour with the ignition fully advanced. If you have to change gear before the first lamp-post, and if the engine knocks, then you know that it requires attention. The time has probably come when it needs decarbonizing, or perhaps there is a loss of compression and the valves need reseating.

How to correct these troubles is dealt with in another part of this book.

After they have been corrected, or at any time after the car has been overhauled, it should then be taken over the test hill again to see if the overhaul has been satisfactory.

Coming down the hill you can test your brakes for proper adjustment. Either brake should be able to hold the car at a standstill on the steepest point of the hill.

In carrying out these tests one should allow for weather conditions. You cannot expect the car to put up the same performance on a wet and heavy surface as on a dry surface. You should not test with a following wind one day and a head wind the next.

Apart from the test hill you can also use the worst road in your district to test for body squeaks and rattles.

OILING AND GREASING

When you receive delivery of your car the maker will present you with a wonderful chart which shows you how to oil and grease it.

The process is comparatively simple, especially if a grease gun is supplied with which to do the work. But even so it is as well to have some sort of system.

If oiling and greasing is done in a haphazard way it is very easy to omit an important bearing which is suffering from thirst.

Under-oiling is one of the worst forms of ill-treatment of a car.

Even if a grease gun is supplied do not attempt to do the job in your best suit. By the time you have finished it will no longer be your best. Put on your worst suit or, better still, overalls.

Put the car in a position where you can manœuvre round it comfortably. Then, armed with your grease gun and oilcan, start with the off front side of the car and work right the way round, following carefully the maker's chart of instructions. This chart should give the correct type of oil and grease to be used for the various parts of the car.

Do not forget that there are also greasers under the bonnet and that the magneto and dynamo occasionally require a spot of oil. There are also greasers under the foot-boards.

Even with the elaborate charts supplied by the makers important parts which require oil are occasionally omitted.

These include brake-rod joints and pins, the accelerator pedal, ignition and other controls, the hinges and locks of the doors, the steering column, and the hinges of the hood struts.

NIGHT DRIVING

Night driving presents rather a difficult set of problems to that of day driving. The beginner on his first night drive should exercise more than ordinary care.

Objects on the road look very different at night, distance is more difficult to judge, and there is a new horror for the motorist, namely, dazzle head-lights.

One advantage of night driving, however, is that your head lights, if they are powerful, act as a warning at cross-roads and round bends. In fact, a good head light at night usurps the function of the horn. Its rays can be seen for a very long distance, and a man coming out of a side turning on to the main road is warned of the approach of a car by its lights.

In fact, in my view, it is safer to drive on a pitch dark night than on a night of semi-darkness.

Twilight Dangers.—The most dangerous time for driving is at twilight. Shortly after the official lighting up time and before real darkness has set in objects become distorted and lamps, however powerful, are dimmed by the half light. Fast driving under such circumstances is folly.

In country districts, in this light, animals and vehicles often assume the same colour as the road. Sheep and cows are very difficult to pick out.

Recently I very nearly ran into a farm labourer who was driving a dun-coloured mule harnessed to a dun-coloured cart. The labourer's clothes were also of the same colour. The whole outfit harmonized well with the colour scheme of the road, and it was not until I almost hit the nose of the mule that this strange apparition became visible.

He carried no lights. You must allow for such breaches of the law in country districts.

While cyclists do not carry rear lights they too are a constant source of menace during twilight. Keep a careful look-out for them.

Dazzle Lights.—In regard to dazzle lights the question of whether to switch off or not is a very difficult one ; it is a problem which has divided motorists into two different camps.

It has led to confusion, bad temper, and very often an exchange of insults.

The chaos of the present conditions is simply killing the old courtesy of the road.

Personally I think it is best for all vehicles to keep on their lights. If you avoid looking at the approaching head lights you do not get the glare. You also have time to see if there is any object on the road between you and the approaching vehicle.

If you keep your head lights on, the moment you pass the approaching motor-car you at once have a clear vision ahead, that is, if you have not looked into the lamps.

If, however, the approaching driver switches off, then I think it is wise to return the compliment. It means that you are blinding him, and that he is nervous. In such cases, for your own safety, it is wise to switch off and go slow.

The spot light is useful as an anti-dazzle device, and there are also numerous anti-dazzle lamps and dimming devices on the market.

But these are not much use unless they are generally adopted. New laws in regard to dazzle lights are shortly expected ; they are certainly needed. People I always switch my lights off for are : motor omnibus drivers, and the drivers of heavy lorries.

Until the problem is tackled by our legislators all motorists should combine in the exercise of extreme care in night driving.

I have been looking over the list of the cases during the past year where dazzle lights have been responsible for accidents. This is a heavy and disturbing list.

ADVENTURING ABROAD

Britain is a beautiful country for touring ; in fact I know of no more beautiful ; but the time comes when we have explored the whole of our own country and we become desirous of seeking fresh fields of adventure.

Taking the car abroad is certainly an adventure, but it is by far and away the best method of seeing new countries.

For one thing, you can get off the beaten track of the ordinary tourist, and you can get among scenery which the railways have to avoid owing to engineering problems connected with railway construction.

But a long European tour should not be undertaken too light-heartedly. The person who sets off without taking any precautions and fancies that he can career unchecked across Europe will quickly be disillusioned.

There are such things as customs and custom's officials.

Unless the tourist is properly equipped he will find it necessary to carry sacks of bullion in his car to negotiate the custom barriers. However, all difficulties of foreign touring can be overcome by placing yourself unreservedly in the hands of the Automobile Association, Whitcomb Street, or of the Royal Automobile Club. These admirable institutions take all responsibility from your shoulders and act as nurse to you and your car.

It is not necessary for me here to state how it is

done. A letter or a personal call to the R.A.C. or A.A. will produce all the information required.

The club will give you, on payment of a deposit, the magic pass which will carry you through all the custom barriers.

Courteous officials will meet you at the ports of departure and landing, and will help you to overcome the ordinary difficulties which arise at this stage of the journey.

Unless you are a very hardy motorist it is also well to find out what parts of Europe are suitable for touring purposes.

The following summary of the present touring conditions in European countries which was prepared for me by the Foreign Touring expert of the R.A.C. will prove useful as a guide :

France.—There is not very much touring in the northern portions of France, but a fair number of people explore Normandy and Brittany and the Château of the Loire, making Tours their headquarters.

Savoy, Dauphiny, and the Pyrenees are favourite touring centres. During the winter months the Riviera is also a very popular touring field. Many people also make the journey down to the Riviera by car.

It is a wonderful journey, the gradual change from the grey northern provinces to the sun-bathed country of the south is too delightful for words, and the first glimpse of the blue Mediterranean alone makes the journey worth while.

Taking the French roads generally, however, they are not so good as could be desired, but according to recents reports a good deal of metal has been deposited by the roadside all over the country, and it is hoped that repairs will soon be perfected.

Belgium.—The battle-field areas still hold an attraction. Many of the roads, however, are bad, although the work of repairing them is being pushed forward. At the same time, bad roads are fully in keeping with the local colouring.

Holland.—A delightful touring country when the bulb fields have carpeted the country with colour. Generally speaking, the roads are fair to good.

Spain.—The roads from the French frontier at San Sebastian along to north of Oviedo and south to Madrid via Burgos, Valladolid, present no difficulties at all.

South of the capital they are, generally speaking, poor, and the roads through the eastern provinces, especially in the direction of Barcelona, should be avoided altogether.

Portugal.—A country with a delightful climate but appalling roads.

Italy.—The roads in the north of the country are fair to moderate. They are good in summer but very dusty. Those in the south are bad.

Switzerland.—This is a wonderful little country in which to tour during the summer months.

The roads are good, but are subjected to some restrictions ; these are gradually being removed.

Germany.—The roads, generally speaking, are good, but touring is comparatively seldom undertaken there at the present time, in consequence of the political and military situation.

Austria and *Czecho Slovakia.*—Here the roads are fair. British motorists are welcome.

Scandinavia.—In Norway the roads are good. In Sweden they are better ; in fact many of the Swedish roads are excellent. In Denmark the roads present no difficulties.

TAKE PLENTY OF SPARES

When taking your car abroad, unless it is of the popular massed produced American variety, it must be remembered that spare parts will be difficult to obtain. If you have not plenty of spares with you, you may be held up for a long period until these are sent out from home, that is, if you are at all off the beaten track.

If your car has been in service for some time you will probably know the parts that are likely to give trouble. As you will be travelling probably over bumpy roads, it is advisable to carry a spare front spring and a spare rear spring. Two spare wheels are also an asset. Among the other spares required, in addition to the ordinary normal spares carried on a British tour, are spare valves and springs, and spare belts or chains for the dynamo and fan drives. A capacious emergency petrol tank is also an advantage.

MOTOR-CAR INSURANCE

The chief point to consider when insuring the car is not so much the question of the premium asked but the record of the insurance company for claim settling.

So many people are inclined to start by collecting an immense store of motor insurance advertisements.

They go through them and say, " I save ten shillings here, one pound on this one, and thirty shillings on this," and select the one on which they save thirty shillings. This is all to the good provided the company are generous when it comes to the test of sound insurance, that is, claim settling.

It is as well to discover, if possible from friends who have had experience, if the company with whom you intend to insure is reliable, if they are well spoken of in regard to settling claims, and what sort of appeal there is if you are unsatisfied in regard to a claim.

If you belong to a motoring association, as you

should do, then it is probably the wisest plan to do your insurance through that association.

The Automobile Association, for instance, will insure its members if required. If you conduct your insurance through them and you have a dispute and your claim is reasonable, then you have the powerful backing of this association.

Also in connexion with the A.A. and Motor Union policies there is a fund amounting to about £20,000 which can be called upon in cases of real hard luck which are not legally covered in the insurance policy. Most insurance policies contain a clause whereby in the case of dispute the matter shall be submitted to arbitration in accordance with the provision of the Arbitration Act. So far so good. But this is often a somewhat expensive procedure. The law is always an expensive luxury.

Under the A.A. policies, in addition to the arbitration clause the Association has an optional right to appeal to a committee of the Association, the members of which are entirely independent of the Insurance Company. This committee considers all cases impartially and their decision is final and binding on the company.

As far as possible legal formalities are dispensed with.

This committee has the power to make grants in cases of hardship referred to above out of the special fund.

Here is a case in point : A motor-car on the main road approaches a side road. A cyclist emerges, rendering it necessary for the motor-car driver to jam on his brakes. In doing so he imposes severe strain on the car, possibly doing it severe damage.

Unless the assured is covered against mechanical breakdown, which probably adds another twenty per cent to the premium, he cannot claim.

In view of the fact, however, that he has probably saved life through his action it would be a case for special treatment and his claim would be settled out of the fund.

Of course the insurance of a motor-car is a matter of one's own personal views on insurance generally.

Some people are quite content to take risks, but I do think that even if a man does not insure his car he is utterly foolish if he does not protect himself by insuring against third-party claims.

The motor-car owner-driver should remember that it is not necessarily his own follies that get him into trouble on the road, but the follies of others. A man who is not insured against third-party risks may find himself keeping a widow or orphaned children for the rest of his life. I know of one particular case where a young man was completely *ruined* by failing to insure against third-party risks.

His lack of foresight in this respect cost him £1,000 at a time when he was beginning to make good.

There is another point in connexion with insurance, and that is whether it is best to stand the smaller risks yourself by agreeing to pay for minor damages up to £10. By so doing it is possible to get a substantial reduction in your premium.

Personally, I consider that it is wiser not to take advantage of this reduction.

Smaller accidents are the more likely accidents.

I do not know what the actuaries say about this, but I feel certain from observation and practical experience that it pays to be insured against such mishaps as smashed mudguards, broken wind-screens, damaged radiators, and so forth.

WIRELESS AND THE CAR

No modern book on motoring would be complete without mentioning the possibilities of wireless in connexion with the motor-car.

The motor-car can of course be used as a means of conveying your ordinary wireless set to a desirable spot where you can listen in, or you can convert your car into a " wireless car."

It is not always feasible to use an ordinary wireless set for listening in while the car is running.

For this purpose a special form of aerial is an advantage, and it is also wise to insulate your wireless set against the bad influences of the magneto and the sparking plugs. Unless these are properly insulated satisfactory results cannot be expected.

For some years the Marconi Company has been experimenting with a view to discovering the most satisfactory means for protecting the wireless set against the influence of the car's ignition. The problem has now been solved.

For the information in this article I am indebted to the motor wireless expert of the Marconi Company, who personally assisted in the conducting of these experiments.

I have myself listened-in to some very delightful concerts while travelling at forty miles per hour or more on the open road.   On a long and tiring journey, such as a run to Scotland, listening-in is a very delightful interlude.

You should, for satisfactory results, have an instrument with a range of at least fifty miles.   This will enable you, on a journey, say, to Scotland, to be within reach, practically the whole way, of at least one of the Broadcasting Stations.

The Marconi Company have found that the most satisfactory wireless instrument is an eight-valve set. The best type of aerial for both closed and open cars is an elevated plate, that is, a sheet of metal slung as high as possible above the car.

In a closed car this sheet of metal can be built into the roof, hung on top of the roof, or slung over the roof.

In the case of the open car it can be fixed to the hood and arranged to close and open with the hood. A frame aerial is possible, but the principal objection to it is that on the open road a motor-car is constantly changing direction. This means that the direction of the aerial has also to be constantly changed.

For insulating the magneto special metal boxes can be obtained which fit over the magneto, and the wire leads to the magneto.

Special insulated sparking plugs can also be obtained.

The motor wireless set should have the least possible number of controls. In the case of closed cars a good position for the set is under the driver's seat. The switchboard and the telephone receivers can be fitted into a panel inside the car. With the Marconi motor wireless set the control consists of only one handle.

The objection to a three- or four-valve set is that such instruments need very delicate operation—not an easy matter when travelling over bumpy roads.

It is advisable to have special batteries for the wireless set. The ordinary battery on your car has sufficient work to do without putting this extra strain on it.

If your car is fitted with a dynamo, a silencer should be obtained, which cuts out any electrical noise. While the dynamo may appear perfectly silent, unless it is new and in irreproachable condition, it will probably set up electrical noises which will disturb the efficient working of your wireless set.

From the above it will be seen that for really good results on a motor-car travelling at speed, the best possible instrument is required.

There is no reason, however, why the amateur should not experiment with a cheaper set.

A.A. ROAD DANGER SIGNS